SNIFFER DOGS

BY ELISABETH NORTON

Apex is distributed by North Star Editions:
sales@northstareditions.com | 888-417-0195

Produced for Apex by Red Line Editorial.

Photographs ©: Shutterstock Images, cover, 8–9, 10–11, 12, 13, 14–15, 18–19, 24, 25, 26–27, 29; iStockphoto, 1, 16–17, 20, 21, 22–23; Eric Talmadge/AP Images, 4–5; USDA Photo/Alamy, 6, 7

Library of Congress Control Number: 2022912234

ISBN
978-1-63738-427-5 (hardcover)
978-1-63738-454-1 (paperback)
978-1-63738-507-4 (ebook pdf)
978-1-63738-481-7 (hosted ebook)

Printed in the United States of America
Mankato, MN
012023

NOTE TO PARENTS AND EDUCATORS

Apex books are designed to build literacy skills in striving readers. Exciting, high-interest content attracts and holds readers' attention. The text is carefully leveled to allow students to achieve success quickly. Additional features, such as bolded glossary words for difficult terms, help build comprehension.

TABLE OF CONTENTS

CHAPTER 1

SNIFFING FOR SNAKES

A dog walks next to an airplane on the island of Guam. He sniffs the air. He is searching for brown tree snakes. These snakes cause many problems on the island.

Guam is an island in the Pacific Ocean. Many brown tree snakes live there.

FAST FACT

Dogs can smell more than 1,000 times better than humans can.

Suddenly, the dog stops. He jumps up and scratches the side of the plane. This action tells his **handler** that he has found a snake.

Dogs check vehicles that go into and out of Guam. They smell if snakes are hiding inside.

Sniffer dogs find thousands of brown tree snakes each year.

Brown tree snakes have already spread to several islands in the Pacific Ocean.

People remove the snake from the plane. That way, the **invasive** snakes won't spread anywhere else.

INVASIVE SNAKES

Brown tree snakes were brought to Guam in the mid-1900s. The snakes spread quickly. They ate many of Guam's birds. By 2015, some kinds of birds had died out completely.

CHAPTER 2

MANY SMELLS

Dogs can learn to detect many different smells. Some sniffer dogs search for plants or animals. They can find food for people to eat. Or they can find pests that hurt plants on farms.

Dogs help people dig for truffles. This food grows underground near tree roots.

Sniffer dogs can also search for dangerous items. For example, some dogs find drugs. Others search for weapons. Their work helps people stay safe.

Police can remove drugs that dogs find.

Some dogs check if people have dangerous items in their cars.

FAST FACT

Dogs can detect bombs and other **explosives**.

In the 2020s, sniffer dogs helped check if people had COVID-19.

Some sniffer dogs can tell when people are sick. These dogs learn what a disease smells like. For example, some dogs can smell cancer.

SNIFFING FOR GERMS

Sniffer dogs can work in hospitals. Some dogs help doctors find what sickness patients have. Others search for germs. They show what places need cleaning.

CHAPTER 3

WHERE DOGS WORK

Some sniffer dogs work with the police. They find stolen or **illegal** items, such as guns or drugs. Dogs also help officers look for people or clues.

Dogs' strong noses can help the police find hidden items.

Sniffer dogs often work at airports, too. The dogs sniff bags and packages. They check for illegal or dangerous items.

FAST FACT

Many sniffer dogs at US airports are beagles. They are called the Beagle Brigade.

At airports, sniffer dogs help find items that are not allowed on planes.

Dogs also help people study the **environment**. These dogs work outdoors. Some dogs find animals. Others look for **scat**. Their work helps scientists do research.

Animal scat can show where animals are living and what they are eating.

Wood turtles are native to North America. But they have begun dying out.

TRACKING TURTLES

Wood turtles are endangered. Sniffer dogs help scientists find them. Scientists put tracking tags on the turtles. Then they set them free. The tags show where each turtle goes.

CHAPTER 4

TRAINING

Each sniffer dog learns to search for a target odor. The dog gets a reward each time it finds this smell.

Sniffer dogs learn to recognize and find certain smells.

For more experienced dogs, trainers may use more scents or more hiding places.

At first, dogs search in a small room. They sniff bags or boxes. They find which one has the target odor. As dogs get better, they search larger areas.

SPECIAL SIGNS

Sniffer dogs give their handlers a sign when they find the target odor. Some dogs sit or lie down. Others bark or scratch.

Dogs may lie down near where the target odor is hidden.

Sniffer dogs' training usually takes 6 to 13 weeks. If dogs pass tests, they can start working. They continue training, too.

FAST FACT

Sniffer dogs usually work until they are six to nine years old. Older dogs often retire.

Sniffer dogs work in more than 60 countries around the world.

COMPREHENSION QUESTIONS

Write your answers on a separate piece of paper.

1. Write a few sentences describing how sniffer dogs are trained.

2. Would you want to be a sniffer dog handler? Why or why not?

3. How much better can dogs smell than humans?

    A. more than 10 times better

    B. more than 100 times better

    C. more than 1,000 times better

4. How would using dogs to search for weapons help people stay safe?

    A. People can remove the weapons before anyone uses them.

    B. People can sell the weapons.

    C. Dogs can take apart the weapons.

5. What does **detect** mean in this book?

Dogs can learn to detect many different smells. Some sniffer dogs search for plants or animals.

    A. try to eat
    B. run away from
    C. look for and find

6. What does **retire** mean in this book?

Sniffer dogs usually work until they are six to nine years old. Older dogs often retire.

    A. keep working
    B. stop working
    C. start training

Answer key on page 32.

GLOSSARY

endangered
In danger of dying out forever.

environment
The natural surroundings of living things.

explosives
Devices that can blow up, such as bombs.

handler
A person who works with and trains an animal.

illegal
Against the law.

invasive
Spreading quickly in a new area and causing many problems there.

patients
People who visit doctors or get other types of medical care.

scat
Animal poop.

BOOKS

Laughlin, Kara L. *Search-and-Rescue Dogs*. New York: AV2 by Weigl, 2019.

Peterson, Megan Cooley. *Eco Dogs*. Minneapolis: Bearport Publishing, 2022.

Peterson, Megan Cooley. *Medical Detection Dogs*. Minneapolis: Bearport Publishing, 2021.

ONLINE RESOURCES

Visit www.apexeditions.com to find links and resources related to this title.

ABOUT THE AUTHOR

Elisabeth Norton is from the United States, but she lives in Switzerland. She teaches English and writes books and poetry. She once met a member of the Beagle Brigade at an airport. His target odor was fruit. He could tell Elisabeth ate an orange for breakfast on the plane!

INDEX

ANSWER KEY:
1. Answers will vary; 2. Answers will vary; 3. C; 4. A; 5. C; 6. B